Also by Rebecca J. Bastian
~*~
The Spirit of America: Back to Basics

Crater Lake Lodge

THROUGH THE KITCHEN DOOR

an exposé

Crater Lake Lodge

THROUGH THE KITCHEN DOOR

an exposé

REBECCA J. BASTIAN

Crater Lake Lodge: Through the Kitchen Door
Second Edition
Copyright © 2024 by Rebecca J. Bastian
Cover design © 2024 by J.P. Biddlecome

All rights reserved. No part of this publication may be reproduced, stored in a retrieval system, or transmitted in any form or by any means electronic, mechanical, photocopying, recording, or otherwise without the prior written permission of the self-published author.

Some names and identifying details have been changed to protect the privacy of individuals.

Although the author and editor have made every effort to ensure that the information in this book was correct at press time, the author and editor do not assume and hereby disclaim any liability to any party for any loss, damage, or disruption caused by errors or omissions, whether such errors or omissions result from negligence, accident, or any other cause.

Original publication Crater Lake Lodge: Through the Kitchen Door.
1st ed. 2020.

ISBN: 978-1-0881-3637-9

For my co-workers.

These are the times that try men's souls.
                              - Thomas Paine

I didn't know he ever worked in a kitchen.

FIRST EDITION PREFACE

I wrote this book because I want people to know the truth about the latest concessionaire at Crater Lake National Park.

Recently out of curiosity I was reading reviews of the Crater Lake Lodge dining room, and I found myself wishing that I could reply to some of these people and explain what things were like behind the scenes.

One reviewer commented that it "obviously wasn't a smooth transition from the previous concessionaire". Congratulations, you've just won understatement of the year.

With a couple exceptions, all of the events related in this book happened during my tenure at the Lodge.

And I have changed the names of all the people and companies involved in order to protect the innocent.

~ Rebecca
2020

SECOND EDITION PREFACE

I still want people to know the truth about the (now previous) concessionaire at Crater Lake National Park. So no more "Tightwad Inc", as I called them in the first edition of this book. From now on I'm going to use their real name.

A lot has been coming to light lately about the way Crater Lake Hospitality, an Aramark subsidiary, treated their employees, Park Service-owned buildings, and the park itself. And so I'm rereleasing this book, with some updates.

Things were bad when I worked there during the 2019 season, but they got even worse after that, with 2023 being the worst year.

SECOND EDITION PREFACE

But in March of 2024, the Park Service finally came to their senses! Aramark was kicked out, and the remainder of their contract was awarded to ExplorUS, a family owned, Kansas based company.

When I first heard about the new company I was skeptical because I had heard that the Park Service apparently allowed Aramark to choose their successor. I wondered if that meant that there was some sort of connection between the two companies. But fortunately, in early May of 2024, I heard from a previous co-worker – who currently has friends working there – and he told me that they're saying things have vastly improved since ExplorUS took over. So hopefully they will continue to do a better job than Aramark. I guess we'll just have to wait and see. For now all I can say is at least Aramark is gone!

~ Rebecca J. Bastian
2024

TABLE OF CONTENTS

A History of Crater Lake..................1

Employees Only..............................5

Glossary..11

    1. Cast of Characters..................15

    2. In the Beginning....................29

    3. Tightwad Inc........................35

    4. If It Ain't Broke, Don't Fix It............41

    5. Chef Jason..........................47

    6. What's on the Menu?..................53

CONTENTS

7. Fun and Games..................................61

8. A Haunting at Crater Lake..................69

9. What Else Could Go Wrong?...............73

10. The Salad that Broke the Camel's Back..77

Afterword..83

Bonus Chapter: The End..................................85

First Edition Acknowledgements....................95

Second Edition Acknowledgements................97

Please Leave a Review....................................99

About the Author..101

Sources..102

A HISTORY OF CRATER LAKE

Crater Lake became a National Park in 1902. The lake was formed a few thousand years ago when Mount Mazama erupted and then collapsed in on itself, forming a caldera which partially filled with rainwater and snowmelt over the years. It's 6 miles across and almost 2,000 feet deep. The lowest point on the rim towers over 500 feet above the surface of the lake. There's also a small mountain within the lake known as Wizard Island, which also has a caldera at the top (but no water in it).

Thanks to its high elevation (over 7,000 feet) Crater Lake has an annual snowfall of about 43 feet, and snowbanks are pretty much a permanent fixture in some places around the rim. It's quite the novelty for visitors to have snowball fights in July.

Because of the lake's varying shades of blue it's known as the jewel of the National Park system. Like most any place, a picture doesn't do it justice, you have to see it with your own eyes to truly appreciate its beauty.

The Park Service takes care of the park, but the concessionaire takes care of the guests. They run the lodge, Annie Creek Restaurant and Gift Shop, the Rim Village Cafe and Gift Shop, the Cabins at Mazama Village, the Mazama Village Store, and Mazama Campground.

Four different concessionaires have had control of these facilities over the years.

The original lodge opened in 1915, but in the early 1990s it was taken apart and rebuilt to be more structually sound, reopening in 1995.

For decades guests have enjoyed a fine dining experience at Crater Lake Lodge, but sadly that changed with the new concessionaire, Aramark.

I've read many reviews that suggest bringing your own food if you're going to be visiting Crater Lake.

EMPLOYEES ONLY

A description of the parts of the lodge that the guests don't see.

<u>THE KITCHEN</u>

Located on the main floor of the lodge, it's separated from the dining room by a hallway that's known as "Server Alley".

In the middle of the kitchen there is an L shaped counter, the long side parallels the back wall, the short side is to the right of the doorway (facing into the kitchen).
The back wall is occupied by (left to right) a sink and small counter, the saute station (stove),

the flat top (industrial-sized griddle), the grill, and the fryer.

The right wall is mostly taken up with a tiny oven, a counter, and the reach-in refrigerator. Next to the refrigerator is the dumbwaiter, and beyond that is the bar area.

The "dish-pit" is on the left side of the kitchen, it consists of a sunken counter (where the dirty dishes go), a sink, the sanitizing machine, and a counter where the clean dishes come out. Next to that is one of the handwashing stations (the other one is on the short side of the "L" on the end nearest the door).

SERVER ALLEY

The servers can access the dining room by one of two doors on either side of the hallway. (This keeps the guests from being able to see into the kitchen.)

On the left side of Server Alley (facing the dining room) is the door to the bar, which was more like a pantry than a bar, and was open to the kitchen on one side.

Hanging on the right side of Server Alley is the 86 board, which was a whiteboard where the cooks would write down what product we were out of, so that the servers knew how to advise the customers. To the right of the 86 board is the door to the stairwell.

PREP KITCHEN

The bottom of the stairway t-bones into a short hallway. Turning right takes you to the main hallway (which snakes it's way throught the rest of the downstairs), and the left takes you to the prep kitchen.

This room is smaller than the main kitchen, probably two thirds or three quarters of its size.

There is a counter in the middle of the room.

Along the back wall is a more primitive dish-pit. No sanitizing machine, just two sinks. One for washing, one for sanitizing.

On the right wall of the prep kitchen are

shelves for storing pans; and a counter containing two more sinks. Next to that is the dumbwaiter. The same one that goes up to the kitchen.

Along the left wall (left to right) is a stove, a small flat top, and a double-decker oven.

To the left of the door (facing the hallway) is a handwashing station, and the door to the walk-in refrigerator. And at the back of the walk-in is the door to the freezer.

DOWNSTAIRS HALLWAY

The main hallway in the basement is long, and slightly slanted and winding. It starts at the service entrance below the dining room and ends at housekeeping's end of the building which contains the elevator banks, and storage for cleaning supplies and linens.

Along the right side (heading towards housekeeping) is the boiler room (or something like that), the dining room manager's office, the EDR (Employee Dining Room), Storage room

#4 which (was also the Chef's office), and the men's restroom.

Turning around at the end of the hallway and heading back you would pass the women's restroom, another stairwell, Storage rooms #5, #3, and #2, the garbage room (Waste Managment), the unisex bathroom, and the short hallway leading to the prep kitchen.

(From the beginning of lodge operations in 1915, garbage was placed outside but that practice attracted black bears, so eventually the Park Service asked that the garbage be kept inside.)

THE STORAGE ROOMS

Storage #5 was for supplies. Gloves, garbage bags, table linens, etc.

Storage #4 was for dry foods, and also for things that don't need refrigeration until after opening.

And as previously mentioned this room also contains an office. There is a desk for the Executive Chef, and one for the Head Chef.

Storage #3 contains one or two reach-ins (for EDR food), and one of the ice machines (the other one is between the unisex bathroom and the hallway to the prep kitchen).

Storage #2 has two reach-ins, a walk-in, and a cart containing flats of bread and hamburger buns.

You may be wondering why I haven't mentioned Storage #1. I believe the walk-in refrigerator and freezer attached to the prep kitchen would technically have been considered Storage #1, I just never heard anyone refer to it as such.

GLOSSARY

To explain some of the terminology of the kitchen.

RUNNING EXPO

This is when a cook or chef stands in the middle of the kitchen and makes sure that the correct dish goes to the correct server. Early on, this person also had to call out the orders from handwritten tickets because the ticket machines (little printers) weren't working yet.

Having an expo can make things run smoother (depending on who it is), but I would argue that they aren't strictly necessary. As long as you put the ticket with the food the servers can look for their name instead of just grabbing dishes willy nilly.

THE WINDOW

No, I'm not talking about drive-thru. "The window" refers to the elevated counter above the cooks' workspace. That's where food goes when it's ready. And if the servers aren't quick enough about coming to collect it, one of the cooks will often yell, "I've got food dying in my window!"

THE LINE

During training I kept hearing people talking about "the line". I finally learned that it refered to the part of the kitchen where the food is actually prepared. It has two parts: The hot side, and pantry.

The hot side is the long side of the L shaped counter that I described before.

GLOSSARY

Pantry (the short side) is where salads, appetizers, and desserts are made. Mostly it is considered the "cold side", except for the tiny oven that was necessary for one of the appetizers and two of the desserts.

FLIPPING

Also known as change-over.

This happened between meal services. For example, after breakfast we would "flip" for lunch. It involved wrapping up the breakfast ingredients, putting them on a cart, and sending them downstairs in the dumbwaiter so they could be taken back to the reach-ins in Storage #2.

Then you'd have to bring up all of the lunch ingredients from downstairs and check to make sure that you had enough of everything.

If you needed more of something you either got the prep cook to get it for you (when we had one), or you had to prep it yourself.

"CORNER!"

That's what you were supposed to say as you were coming around a blind corner, to warn anybody who might be coming the other way, so you wouldn't bump into each other.

CHAPTER 1
CAST OF CHARACTERS

I may have hated my job, but I liked most of my co-workers. Here's a list of names that will reoccur. Names have been changed, except my own.

Some of these characters were temporary chefs sent from other Aramark properties to help us get on our feet. Some were foreign students in the U.S. on a work program. They were known as "J1s".

(Please note that I have not included everyone. Also, I may have forgotten certain facts about some of these people, such as where they are from or if they had previously worked at Crater Lake.)

REBECCA (Me)

Pantry Cook.
From Oregon.
I was hired as a prep cook but I was promoted to pantry cook on opening day. (More about that later.)

WYATT

Lead Cook.
From California.
He was cool.

KIANA

Lead Cook.
From California.

Worked at Crater Lake before for the previous concessionaire.

Sadly she left at the end of June.

LEILANI

Server.

She knew how to cut strawberries into beautiful roses for garnishing desserts.

During training she helped us prep the food that we would need up at the lodge.

She ended up leaving in early July.

JOSEPH

Lead Cook.
From Oregon.
Very hard worker.

ZEKE

EDR Cook.
From Oregon.
He had a handlebar mustache and he sometimes smoked a pipe during his breaks. He also talked kind of slow.

He was always saying "Why do you hate me?" in a high pitched voice. (Eventually all of the J1s started saying it too.) He also liked to ask (in an exagerated Texas drawl), "Wanna be friends?" And he would say "corner" in a funny voice.

Joseph told me this story: He once witnessed an encounter between Zeke and one of the temporary dining room managers. She saw Zeke standing near the door to the bathroom and I guess he was holding a pack of cigarettes, because she asked, "You're not going to smoke in there are you?"

Zeke said he wasn't, but when she walked away he started singing "Smokin' in the Boys Room".

CAST OF CHARACTERS

EDUARDO

Temporary Chef.
He was our first prep cook.
I remember one day of training when Eduardo was trying to read a recipe that another temporary chef had written (who should have been a doctor, going by his handwriting), and he asked one of the other chefs, "Why are we putting tobacco in this dish?"

"It's probably supposed to say tobasco." The other chef replied.

"Ah," said Eduardo, "Yeah, that makes more sense."

ALBERTO

Temporary Chef.
From South Carolina.
He was cool.

CHAZ

Server.
From Nevada.
Everytime he came back to the kitchen with an order it was always "pretty straight forward", even though it almost never was.
He eventually left in the middle of the night without a word to anyone.

BARRY

Server.
Worked at Crater Lake before for the previous concessionaire.
I privately refered to him as Eyore. He talked slow and quiet, and rarely smiled.

PAUL

Server.

From Oregon.
Worked at Crater Lake before for the previous concessionaire.
He was about six and a half feet tall.
He ended up leaving in late July.

MATTIE

Server.
From Oregon.
She was one of my favorite servers, always very understanding.

BEN

Server.
From Colorado.
Worked at Crater Lake before for the previous concessionaire.

OSWALD

Server.
From Texas.
He had a facial tic, was constantly winking and darting his tounge out. I once heard him joke that he was born at a time when they weren't cautioning expectant mothers not to drink.

WILL

Head Chef.
From Louisiana.
He was always worrying (in a funny way) about being on top of a volcano. That, and complaining about all the snow.
He was a good boss. He actually cared about the employees, actually helped us, and actually knew what he was doing.
He quit not long after our Executive Chef showed up. He was greatly missed.

CAST OF CHARACTERS

JONATHAN

Aramark Chef.
He was there at the beginning to see how the opening went, and he came back a couple months later to see how things were going. (I would love to know what he put in his report.)

NATASHA

Pantry Cook (for most of the season).
From Russia.
She and Sonya started out as dishwashers, but after a couple weeks I trained them on pantry.

SONYA

Pantry Cook (for most of the season).
From Russia.
The brilliant HR department conflated her

and Natasha and made one ID card for the two of them. As I recall, they used Sonya's picture, Natasha's first name, and a combination of their last names. (That eventually got straightened out.)

GRANT

Head Chef (for most of the season).
From Oregon.
He was hired as the Sous Chef, but he got promoted when Will quit.
Worked at Crater Lake before for the previous concessionaire, and literally left his mark on the place. He pointed out a couple dents in the wall at the bottom of the stairwell that were caused by him skimming down the stairs too quickly.

BETH

Server.
Zeke's girlfriend.

She was also one of my favorite servers.

THAKSIN

Cook (for most of the season).
From Thailand.
He started out as a dishwasher, but Wyatt asked to train him as a cook because he needed help in the mornings. And I also trained him on pantry so he could help me once in awhile.

He brought some cool refrigerator magnets with him from Thailand as gifts for his co-workers.

RICHARD

Temporary Prep Cook.
From Missouri.
He was *very* polite. Everybody was either Sir or Ma'am.

I can remember going downstairs to the prep kitchen to ask him for diced tomatoes or whatever, and he would say, "I'll get those done right away for you, ma'am."

Ma'am? He had me looking over my shoulder for an older woman. Being unmarried and in my twenties it's a strange feeling for me to be called ma'am.

And it was amusing to hear him address guys younger than him as, sir.

GRIGORY

Busser.
From Russia.
He was a very talented photographer.

MAGGIE

Cocktail Waitress.
From Pennsylvania.
She was fun.

CAST OF CHARACTERS

LOLA

>Cocktail Waitress.
>From Utah.
>She was cool.

ELLIE

>Cocktail Waitress.
>She was nice.

MAY

>Cocktail Waitress.
>She was also nice.

SERKAN

>Cook.
>From Turkey.

He worked at Crater Lake before for the previous concessionaire.

AYLA

Cook.
From Turkey.
I also trained her on pantry, so she was able to help me occasionally.

JASON

Executive Chef.
From California.
You'll meet him later.

CHAPTER 2
IN THE BEGINNING

May 13th.
Orientation was a waste of time. All they talked about was the company's mission statement, obvious safety practices, and the standard lecture about "sustainability".

The only useful thing they taught us was how to handle a dissatisfied customer. (I guess they knew there would be plenty of those.)

But not one peep about how to call in sick. (Since there weren't very many of us maybe they were hoping that we would just come in anyway.)

My last job had been in Arizona working for Xanterra (the company that used to have the Crater Lake contract), and I saw a *big* difference between the two companies.

Xanterra made sure that their employees had a complete list of names and phone numbers, clearly identifying who the managers were for the different departments. And they also made sure that their employees were clear on the call-in procedure.

Aramark did none of that.

WATER WATER EVERYWHERE

I don't know if it was ignorance or arrogance that caused this massive mistake, but in any case Aramark did not winterize the lodge properly (if at all) and the pipes burst.

So, about a week before opening day, managment walked into the building (apparently for the first time since November) and were greeted by holes in the ceiling that were pouring water everywhere. Naturally they had to make major last minute repairs, and as a result we had to do our training in the kitchen at Annie Creek Restaurant.

Then on opening day it was a mad dash to move all of the prepped food 7 miles up the mountain to the lodge, and get all the pots and pans and things out of storage.

DON'T LET THERE BE LIGHT

The light in the walk-in refrigerator at Annie Creek was out, so anybody who needed to get something out of there had to take a flashlight with them.

At first only about half the lights were working in the main kitchen at the lodge, so it was pretty dark in there.

INVISIBLE INK?

You expect recipes to make sense, to list all of the ingredients, to give clear instructions. Well apparently you can't expect that when you're going off a recipe that was written by

Aramark.

During training Chef Alberto had me helping him make the desserts, and we started with the bread pudding.

In reading the instructions I learned that we were supposed to bake the pears. Pears? I reread the ingredients list. No pears.

Fortunately, Alberto possessed the secret knowledge and was able to tell me how many to use and how they should be cut.

I don't understand how that recipe could have been written so poorly. Or why it was expected that a rookie would just *know* what to do.

GOTTA GO

In the rush to get the lodge ready to open, only the bare minimum of plumbing was repaired. So neither the men's room nor the women's room was functioning (at least the toilets weren't). That left only the single toilet unisex bathroom for *everybody*. Grant refered to it as the "disease closet".

TOO MANY CHEFS IN THE KITCHEN

Sometime during the first week at the lodge, Will asked me to cut up the foccacia bread for dinner. He wanted it cut into squares.

But after I'd been doing it that way for awhile, Alberto came along and told me that I should be cutting it into parallelograms instead.

So I did it his way until Jonathan came over and told me that it would look better if it was cut into triangles.

Personally I don't understand why the *shape* of the bread is so important.

THE SCHEDULE

From the beginning I was promised that I would get two days off each week and that only for the first week would I work six days. But when the new schedule came out it only gave me one day off.

"Oh," they said, "you'll get to start the new schedule next week."

And I believed them.

Then the new schedule would be posted. Still only one day.

"Oh," again, "you'll get to start the new schedule next week."

I still believed it.

The new schedule would be posted. One day.

They led me on for weeks like that. And I let them.

CHAPTER 3
TIGHTWAD INC.

Aramark (or Tightwad Incorporated as I like to call them) don't care about their employees or their guests, all they care about is money. And they will cut whatever corners they can in order to spend as little as possible.

BOING

Wyatt was passed over for the first pay period.

HR claimed that there was some issue with his paycheck going through, but they were "working on it".

After being passed over for the second pay period Wyatt walked out during breakfast service. Will talked him back and HR cut a check to hold him over until they could get his actual paycheck.

Wyatt took the check to Medford on his day off and tried to cash it. It bounced. Very odd.

(Eventually Wyatt did get paid.)

OVERWORKED AND UNDERPAID

I applied to be a prep cook, and that's how I was hired, at a rate of $11.25 an hour.

Opening day they promoted me to pantry cook because they hadn't hired one. (And there were supposed to be two.) On top of that they kept my hourly the same.

In mid-July I hit the end of my rope. I'd been working an average of twelve hours a day, six days a week, for nine weeks, at the pay grade of a prep cook. I was fed up with being lied to, and exhausted. So I tried to quit.

But Jonathan talked me out of it by

promising to reduce my hours to something more reasonable. And they did.

My new schedule was a normal forty hour work week with two days off. But I'm sure the only reason I got it was because it meant they wouldn't have to pay me as much. (Later I would find out just how true that was.)

Thanks to a conversation I had with one of the cooks, I found out that I was being cheated.

Pantry cooks were supposed to get $15.00 an hour. Yet from the day that I was "promoted" I was still being paid as a prep cook. So basically I was doing the work of two pantry cooks for the pay of less than one.

I brought this up to Grant and he said he would see what he could do. But of course nothing ever came of it and Aramark still owes me over $2,700 in backpay.

NOT COOL

You would think that the most sensible time

to install new equipment would be before opening or after closing, right? And it would be. But if you're Aramark you have it done between lunch and dinner services.

One day, in the midst of change-over, one of the maintenance guys came upstairs and told Joseph that they were going to bring in the new refrigeration units for the hot side. This was news to Joseph.

So the guys brought up both units and set them in the middle of the room. I had to move back into the bar area so that they could push one of the refrigerators around the corner and get it in position to go under the grill. Joseph and Zeke had to lift the grill off the shelves it had been sitting on and hold it up until the maintenance guys got the new unit into place. The same process was then repeated on the other end of the line at the saute station.

Meanwhile the other cooks had to wait to continue flipping for dinner because the maintenance guys (and the tables that had been replaced) were in the way.

Why on earth did they have to do this now, I

wondered? *Why not wait until dinner is over so they wouldn't be disrupting anything?* The answer occured to me much later. Overtime pay. Had this equipment installation been done after hours, that would have meant Aramark having to pay the maintenance guys time and a half.

By the way, that refrigeration unit that the saute station was sitting on? Not quite big enough. The saute station eventually fell off, and it took three guys to pick it up from the floor. Oh, and they were told that they couldn't weld the saute station to the refrigeration unit because that would void the warranty.

CHAPTER 4
IF IT AIN'T BROKE, DON'T FIX IT

Or something like that.

LEAVE WELL ENOUGH ALONE

They called it the "Nuclear Well". It only had two settings: Off, and extremely hot.

The two wells were deep insets in the counter on the hot side, positioned on the outside so that the servers or expo could get to it without being in the cooks' way. The wells functioned as a double boiler. Pots of oatmeal or soup were set inside them to keep the contents warm.

But due to the nature of the Nuclear Well,

spoons had to be crisscrossed in the bottom in order to keep the pot from touching, or else the contents would burn.

Water also had to be constantly poured into the well. Fortunately it had a built in reminder system. Whenever it ran out of water it would start smoking.

One time, one of the J1s from Turkey misunderstood and poured the soup directly into the well. That was a fun mess that he had to clean up.

THE UPS AND DOWNS

The dumbwaiter is a great invention. It allows you to easily transport heavy things from one floor to the other.

We used ours for everything from food carts, to the ice cambros (wheeled bins), to full bags of garbage.

Of course it wasn't so great when it would get stuck between floors, because then we'd have to carry everything up and down manually.

As I recall it once got stuck while carrying a bag of garbage, and they didn't fix it until morning. You can imagine the smell.

But even when it was working properly it had the potential to give you a workout.

Imagine: Down in the prep kitchen you'd load a food cart or an ice cambro into the dumbwaiter. Close the inner door and the outer door, just like an old fashioned elevator. Push the up arrow and then head upstairs.

But when you get to the kitchen, the light that indicates the presence of the dumbwaiter isn't on. Back down the stairs.

Somebody else needed to use the dumbwaiter and called it down because they didn't realize that you had just sent it up. They are in the process of opening the doors as you come into the prep kitchen. They see whatever it is that you put in there. "Were you sending this up or down?"

"Up."

"Oh. Sorry."

"Yeah."

And so they close the doors again and send the dumbwaiter back up. But not before extracting a promise from you to send it down again after you've pulled your stuff out.

Then there were the times when people would forget and leave it open.

So you'd have to run downstairs, close the doors and push the button, run upstairs to load it, and then run back downstairs to unload it.

One time, when another cook was loading a food cart into the dumbwaiter, while we were flipping for lunch, the remainder of a bag of liquid eggs fell off the cart and poured down the crack between the floor and the dumbwaiter. The cook cleaned up what had gotten on the floor, but there was nothing they could do about the rest of it, except to advise the maintenence crew that they'd have a mess to clean up later. I remember the head maintenence guy saying that they would clean out the dumbwaiter pit at the end of the season, and that they would call it the Crater Lake Omelette.

FRIED

The original fryer was somewhat temperamental. I don't know if it was just old and worn out, or if it was damaged by having water poured on it during the pipe disaster.

It worked off and on for about a month I think, before dying altogether. Then it sat there for another few weeks while Aramark decided if it was worth spending the money to buy a new one.

CHAPTER 5
CHEF JASON

He was a big bald guy, at least six and a half feet tall, maybe more.

My first impression of him was that all he needed was a hockey mask and a machete to complete his look.

WHAT ARE WE OUT OF TODAY?

Once Jason took over ordering food from the restaurant supply company we rarely got everything that we needed. And as a result we were constantly having to 86 menu items. Sometimes we had to have food brought up from Annie Creek, but they couldn't bring us everything.

I felt bad for the servers, always having to make excuses to the customers. For example, telling customers that the truck hadn't come in yet even though it had.

But what was funny was when Jason started telling us that we couldn't 86 stuff. I'm not sure what we were expected to do instead, he never seemed to have any suggestions for that. I would have voted for getting an executive chef that was actually competent at the job.

DUMB, DUMBER, AND DUMBEST

I once heard somebody refer to Jason as the "big dumb S.O.B". This person also once said, "I may not be smarter than a 5th Grader, but at least I'm smarter than Jason". To which I replied, "Who isn't?"

You can see that we held our dear Executive Chef in very high esteem.

NO JOKE

Jason had little to no sense of humor.

I once put a flatbread on the window that was less than perfect, and Jason, who was running expo (fortunately that was extremely rare), looked it over and said, "It's black, we can't serve that."

Kiana replied, "Well that's racist."

I laughed, but the joke went right over Jason's head. "Do another one," he said, "I'm not sending this out."

It was nice to have such a cheerful boss.

FREE ICE CREAM

I don't remember who it was, but eventually someone discovered that Jason was keeping a secret stash of ice cream bars. (These he always remembered to order, even when forgetting critical menu items.) So the employees (mostly the J1s) made a habit of raiding said "secret" stash. And the fact that Jason never said anything about it leads me to believe that he *couldn't* say anything about it.

I'm guessing it was a circle of life kind of thing. Jason would steal from the company, the employees would steal from Jason, and the company would steal from the employees.

HELPING HAND

Jason usually came upstairs from the office to "help out" during dinner service.

His version of helping was to get in the way, point out everything that everybody was doing wrong, flip a couple steaks (occasionally cross contaminating them with the chicken), and brag about making Executive Chef by the time he was thirty (how he managed that I'll never know). Eventually he would find an excuse to go back downstairs for the rest of the night and everybody would breathe a collective sigh of relief.

NO CHEF LEFT BEHIND

Well... maybe just one.

Aramark ran shuttles to Medford and Klamath Falls so that any employee who wanted to could get off the mountain on their day off.

And one time when Jason took the shuttle to Medford, it came back without him. Give that shuttle driver a cigar! Unfortunately they ended up going back for him. Give me back that cigar. (And no, I did not bribe the driver to maroon Jason.)

Apparently the shuttle got all the way back to Crater Lake before anybody noticed that Jason wasn't with them. Or maybe somebody did notice and just chose to keep their mouth shut, I don't know. But I really wish that he had taken that as a sign that he should just buy a plane ticket home.

SOMETHING FISHY

I did not witness the following story but it was repeated to me later.

During one particularly busy dinner service, the cooks ran out of salmon fillets. So one of them (a cook, not a salmon) hurried downstairs to find the ever helpful Executive Chef.

He found Jason mopping the floor (a task of imminent importance), and asked if he would cut up some more salmon and send it upstairs.

Evidently Jason's reply was something along the lines of, "Why can't one of you guys do it?"

What else could he say? After all, the cooks have nothing better to do and the floors won't mop themselves.

A METHOD TO HIS MADNESS

Supposedly Jason confessed to being a former tweaker. Now I didn't hear this directly from him, it was passed on to me by someone else, but it wouldn't surprise me if it was true. A meth addiction would explain a lot about his behavior.

CHAPTER 6
WHAT'S ON THE MENU?

According to the lodge website, the chefs' "gourmet creations" are made with ingredients grown in Oregon.

I don't know about that, but I do know that they got everything from CheapCo, a restaurant supply company.

Now maybe all that stuff did come from Oregon, but unfortunately I can't say for sure becuase my research was not conclusive one way or the other.

CheapCo is happy to tell you that their product is "sustainable", but they're not real big on telling you where they source it.

GLUTEN FREE

The customer is not always right. Sometimes there are customers who order food just so they can complain about it, because it gets them attention. The week after opening we had just such a customer.

This woman ordered the vegetarian dish, which the menu clearly states contains barley.

When Ben went back to check the water after he had delivered the food, the customer demanded to talk to the Chef. So Ben came back to the kitchen to get Will.

Evidently the woman told Will that everything was great, but proceeded to complain again the next time Ben stopped by.

When he came back to the kitchen he relayed what she had said: "There's gluten in this barley! It'll stay in my system for forty-five days! Now I have to go take a pill!"

Kiana told him to smack the woman.

Ben replied that the husband was sitting right there.

Kiana said to hit him, too.

Will's idea was to tell the woman that there was a tree outside she could chew on.

I know it doesn't seem very nice to make fun of someone who apparently has celiac disease, but I don't believe that she really did. Because wouldn't you think someone who truly had a problem with gluten for health reasons would pay closer attention to the ingredients list on a menu? Her behavior suggests to me that she was simply an attention seeker.

HAVE A LITTLE PASTA WITH YOUR GARLIC

People who smoke have a hard time tasting salt. Apparently this also applies to smelling garlic.

I remember one time when Wyatt was working saute during lunch service. He was in the process of making one of the pasta dishes. Jonathan, who was standing next to him, asked if he thought he had put enough garlic in it. He was being facetious. The smell of garlic was overpowering to me and I was standing about ten feet away.

I pity whoever ordered that pasta.

WINGING IT

When the cooks saw the menu at the beginning of the season, we couldn't believe it. Crater Lake Lodge was going to be serving hot wings. If Aramark was so deadset on serving wings, they should have had them on the menu at Annie Creek (a casual, buffet style restaurant). The lodge is supposed to be a high end restaurant, not a sports bar.

Of course as it worked out we had to 86 them most of the time because of the situation with the fryer. And when we finally got a new one, the availability of the wings depended on whether Jason ordered them or not. I read one review that said the person was told that the wings were not available because they were so popular. Right...

IN A PICKLE

One of the appetizers was a shrimp and pickled vegetable dish.

On our last day of training we made and tasted all of the food that we would be serving at the lodge. After trying this particular dish Kiana cautioned me to eat it over a trash can. It wasn't quite that bad, but I certainly wouldn't pay $12 for it, especially since the serving size is only about a cup full.

FAST FOOD

Imagine a chocolate cake with a molten center and a side of Chantilly Cream. Doesn't that sound good? Well, maybe not.

So do yourself a favor and get it from Jack-in-the-Box instead, they're much cheaper there. (Aramark and Jack-in-the-Box ordered the same premade lava cakes from CheapCo).

Of course they don't serve it with Chantilly Cream, but then neither did we.

Now maybe they changed things after I left, but during my time there we always used plain old whipped cream out of the can.

"LOCAL"

All the salads were described as being made with "local" lettuce. That makes it sound as though it was picked fresh from the farmer's field doesn't it? Instead it was picked fresh from the cellophane bag that came from CheapCo, at the other end of the state.

"HANDCUT" RIBEYE

Maybe it was, but not at the lodge. They came individually packaged from CheapCo.

Except of course for the time when they didn't arrive at all. (Because you-know-who forgot to order them.)

The company had to send somebody all the way to Medford to buy a whole bunch of steaks from a big-box store.

TRUCK STOP VINTAGE

At one point the bar ran out of wine, so our temporary dining room manager gave some money to one of the servers so that they could go buy a couple of bottles from the travel center near Chiloquin. At thirty miles distant, it was the closest source.

I'm pretty sure Chateau Gas Station wasn't added to the wine list. Anyway, at least it was bottled and not boxed.

BAG FOR YOUR SOUP?

I read one review that said something about the soup tasting like it came out of a can. I'm sorry, but I have to correct you on that. It actually came out of a bag.

That's right, CheapCo's fingerprints were on the soup as well. They made it, all we did was pour the contents of the bag into the pot in the soup well to keep it warm.

It also said in that review that the soup was barely warm, as though it had only been briefly microwaved. And it probably was.

There were a couple times when servers would spoon out soup that had just been put into the pot, so it hadn't had the chance to get warm yet. And in those instances they usually would microwave it for about a minute. Evidently that wasn't enough.

THE OLD DAYS

According to Kiana the previous concessionaire's Executive Chef actually had tastebuds. Evidently they used to serve things like Elk and Filet Mignon.

But of course that's not as classy as hot wings.

CHAPTER 7
FUN AND GAMES

If you were to ask me what I missed about this job, I would have to say the antics that went on in the kitchen. You have to be crazy to survive seasonal work. And I mean that in the nicest possible way.

The seemingly endless monotony, even when broken up by disasters, can be soul-numbingly depressing. (I often heard some of my coworkers compare it to the movie *Groundhog Day*.) So you have to take your fun where you can find it.

NUTTY

Wyatt liked to mess with Paul during

breakfast service.

For example: Paul would come back asking if his order of pancakes was ready yet.

"What pancakes?" Wyatt would ask.

"The ones I ordered. Didn't you get the ticket?"

"No, I'm sorry, I guess it didn't come through."

When I would look through the window I could see Wyatt trying unsucessfully to hold back a smirk, so I would inform Paul that Wyatt was just messing with him.

Paul's response was to pick up the walnuts that were meant for oatmeal topping and start chucking them at Wyatt.

Wyatt would laugh and finally put the food in the window.

MUSIC FESTIVAL

Heavy Metal, Rap, Country, Pop (American, Russian, and Turkish), Disney soundtracks, you name it, we probably played it.

(Grant once asked if anybody had heard of Country Rap. He said it's called Crap.)

Some of the cooks brought their own bluetooth speakers (Will actually gave us his before he left), but it seemed like everybody liked to use Joseph's for some reason.

They abused the privilege and used it until it gave out. Surprisingly it gave out from constant use and not from the one time Ayla accidently dropped it into the pork juice.

And when Joseph eventually had to buy a new one he did not share it.

One time during closing when Kiana was singing along to her music, one of the servers came back to tell her that the few remaining customers could hear her and they said that she had a good voice. Kiana jokingly offered to go out and serenade them.

NICKNAMES

Will loved giving people nicknames.

Natasha and Sonya were "Chip and Dale" because you rarely saw one without the other.

Wyatt had two nicknames. He was either "Sensei" or "Spaz", depending on whether he was on the ball or not.

The origins of my nickname are a little more abstract.

I was late for work the Saturday before Memorial Day because I failed to anicipate how bad the traffic would be. On a normal day, it would take about five minutes from the Mazama dorm driveway to the park entrance station. But that day the line of cars was so long it took an hour and a half. And with no way to contact anyone I couldn't warn them that I would be late. So when I finally made it to the lodge Will started teasing me about being distracted in the woods like the dog from the movie *UP*.

And from then on Will would yell "Squirrel!"

when he wanted to get my attention. Wyatt and Joseph eventually started doing it too. And that evolved into my nickname: Squirrel.

WHIPPED CREAM

One of Ayla's favorite things to do was to spray whipped cream on her palm, sneak up behind Serkan and smack him in the face.

Maggie and Ayla often played the whipped cream challenge: You spray whipped cream on the back of your hand then smack your arm to bounce the whipped cream into the air and try to catch it in your mouth.

Niether of these things were a very responsible use of our limited supply of whipped cream, but I wasn't going to be the one to tell them not to do it.

FOOD FACES

A couple of times Natasha and Sonya played with leftover food and made little faces:

FUN AND GAMES

Finding these always made my day a little brighter.

CHAPTER 8
A HAUNTING AT CRATER LAKE

Some strange things happened in the kitchen (besides Jason's behavior). I only have a definite explanation for one event:

There was a wallphone in the kitchen that we were told didn't work. So it was rather startling when it rang one day.

"Didn't you know?" Joseph joked, "We're doing takeout now."

I answered it and couldn't hear anything, so I hung up.

We learned later that one of the maintenance guys had been attempting to fix the phone in the prep kitchen and that mysterious call had simply been a test. He could hear me but I couldn't hear him.

I don't think they ever did get that phone back to being a two-way.

SHATTERED GLASS

Duties of the table bussers included polishing the clean glasses and putting them away. They would often do this at the table next to pantry.

One day during Grigory's turn, something unusual happened. A glass broke. It was just sitting on the table, nobody was touching it. CRACK! Just like somebody had squeezed it too hard. Grigory and I looked at each other, puzzled.

Probably a hairline crack had been developing and just happened to reach its breaking point at that moment. But that incident was still rather strange.

FLYING SPATULA

This I have no explanation for. I've never seen anything like it.

I was standing behind the pantry counter and Wyatt was on the other side of the kitchen washing his hands. Out of the corner of my eye I saw movement and quickly turned my head. The spatula that had been sitting at the back of the flat top was flying through the air. When it hit the floor Wyatt turned to look for the source of the sound. I stepped over to the hot side to see if anyone was playing some kind of elaborate practical joke. (Serkan would often sit on the floor back there when there wasn't anything going on, so I thought maybe it was him.) But there was nobody there, just the spatula laying on the floor. Wyatt and I looked at each other with wide eyes.

It honestly looked as though someone (an invisible someone) had picked up the spatula and tossed it over their shoulder. It definitely didn't *fall* off as it was at least a foot and a half from the edge of the flat top.

Unfortunately I was the only one who saw it actually fly through the air. This was one time that I wished there were security cameras in the kitchen.

CHAPTER 9
WHAT ELSE COULD GO WRONG?

It began with the health inspection by the National Park Service affiliated health inspectors; the military grade, white glove inspection.

Basically they came in and told us that we were doing several things wrong. (There's a shocker.)

- The refrigeration unit under the pantry counter wasn't holding temperature, and neither were the ones on the hot side.
- The garbage room was dirty. (No, really?)
- We had a fly problem. (Because of the

garbage room.)
- The soap dispenser at the pantry handwashing station wasn't the right kind. (So one of the maintenance guys installed one. And it interfered with opening the door of the refrigeration unit.)
- There were dust bunnies under the equipment on the hot side. (Last time I checked we weren't cooking things *under* the flat top.) This same complaint was made about the prep and EDR kitchens.

So we failed our first inspection, but they wouldn't close us down. Instead they gave us time to correct our mistakes. We were told to expect a second inspection (not when, of course). Fun times.

Following that revelation we all got the lecture from Jason about how we needed to make sure that we passed the next time. I remember him saying that it was important to pass because if we failed again he could lose his job. Apparently he believed that we would think that was a bad thing.

4TH OF JULY FIASCO

I'm not sure what the servers said to the customers that day. Maybe something like this: "Do you know what you would like for lunch? We have salad, salad, or salad."

So it turns out that running out of food isn't as bad as not having the ability to *cook* the food.

Just as breakfast service was ending Wyatt discovered that we were out of propane. This just had to happen on the 4th of July.

And for once we had a problem that could not be blamed on Jason or Aramark. No, this rested solely on the gas company that was supposed to come fill our propane tank every week. Needless to say, they forgot this time.

And until the truck came we couldn't serve anything but salads, appetizers, and desserts. So we turned the entire kitchen into pantry and all the cooks pitched in.

Fortunately for the cooks also working dinner, the propane was back on by then.

WAITER?

When a guy in a grimy shirt, with a huge ring of keys hooked to his belt comes out to wait on your table you know something must be wrong.

One fine day not long after the fourth, the servers who were supposed to be working lunch decided to stage a walkout. Replacements were called in, but they all lived down the mountain at Mazama dorm. So in the meantime, management and maintenance had to step in and wait on the guests.

That was probably the funniest disaster that I ever witnessed. Funny to me anyway. I can only imagine what the guests thought.

We found out later that the reason the servers were mad was because we didn't have anybody to run expo. I'm sorry, but that was the least of our problems in that place.

CHAPTER 10
THE SALAD THAT BROKE THE CAMEL'S BACK

The crap really started to hit the fan after Grant talked me out of quitting for the third time.

A CUT ABOVE THE REST

July 15th.
I never knew that avacados could be so dangerous. But with the wrong kind of knife, this particular one was.

CRATER LAKE LODGE -THROUGH THE KITCHEN DOOR

When I was a kid my Dad showed me how to take the pit out of an avacado: You cut all the way around it longways, then twist the two halves apart. Hold the half containing the pit in one hand, then with your knife you whack the pit and twist it out.

I'd done this hundreds of times with no problem. But on this occasion all the paring knives that I usually used were in the dish-pit. And in that hurried environment I couldn't wait for the correct tool, so I reached for the only knife that was left. Unfortunately when I was attempting to whack the pit the knife slipped and went right through the avacado into the base of my middle finger. I didn't really feel it, I just knew that it was too far into the avacado to have missed my hand.

The avacado had to be tossed, obviously, because nobody wants blood on their appetizers. And that knife too had to go to the dish-pit. Meanwhile I hurried downstairs to the First Aid station and attempted to bandage my hand.

Unfortunately I ended up needing stitches (which hurt worse than getting cut). And even though I filled out all the workers compensation paperwork (and was assured that there wouldn't be any problem), I eventually got a letter saying that Aramark's insurance provider wouldn't pay my over $300 medical bill. But they wouldn't say why. And I was never given a claim number, so I couldn't check up on it.

I have to wonder if Jason ever actually sent in the paperwork.

THE EXPLOSION

August 1st: (The same day that the new refrigeration units were put in.)

Jason came upstairs near the end of my shift and immediatly started complaining about the wilted lettuce in the side salad station.

"We can't serve that!"

Well we weren't serving it, lunch had been over for awhile at that point. But even though I had some help that afternoon I hadn't gotten around to cleaning up the side salad station yet because of all the commotion with the equipment installation (which, by the way, was Jason's brilliant idea). Before I could explain, he told me that I "needed" to be doing the side salads myself, that the wait staff shouldn't, even as they were waiting for them. At that moment I was busy prepping for dinner, mostly by myself, and had no time to worry about the leftover salad from lunch.

"No," I said, "I don't have the time."

Jason demanded to know why then were Natasha and Sonya able to do it.

I proceeded to reminded him (in a much louder voice than I usually used) that there were two of them while I was by myself most of the time. Additionally the servers preferred to take one salad at a time instead of waiting on me to prep the salads for them.

He told me that I couldn't talk to him that way.

"I'll talk to you however *I* want to!"

He sent me home after this exchange. I guess that was supposed to be some kind of punishment. But I was glad to get a break.

(I was later praised by a couple of my co-workers for standing up to Jason.)

THE NOTE

August 6th: Third day of work after the explosion.

The first thing I saw upon coming up to the kitchen was a note, written in permanent marker on a piece of cardboard, taped to the door of the reach-in. It was supposedly from Natasha and Sonya, but I know who it was really from.

The note began with "Dear Rebecca", and then it went on to tell me that I had to do all the side salads myself. It also told me that I had to keep the reach-in better organized.

I never will understand why Jason kept insisting that I was some kind of superhuman who could do the work of two people, without help.

So, I ripped the note off the reach-in, chucked it into the recycle pile, and proceeded to go about my usual set-up routine for lunch service. Unfortunately, Grant stopped me as I was setting up the side salad station and made me do it Jason's way.

That's when I finally saw the writing on the wall; things were just getting worse in that place, and it wouldn't improve. Aramark was never going to fork over a corrected paycheck, I was never going to get permanent help, and there was no one in a position of power who could, or would, do anything about either of those things. So this pantry cook – still being paid prep cook wages – worked her final shift that day.

AFTERWORD

I read several reviews in which the commenters said that they wouldn't come back until Aramark was gone. Some reviewers also said that they were already aware of the company's reputation and were not surprised.

This reputation was acquired by serving less than quality food, by refusing to award backpay to employees who were underpaid, and by firing employees who reported the company for unsanitary conditions.

Evidently the Park Service was *not* aware of Aramark's reputation when they accepted their bid to be the concessionaire for Crater Lake (and for fourteen other National Parks). But in any case that company is driving away visitors, and not only is that a sad fact in itself, but sooner or

AFTERWORD

later it could effect the local economy. The Park Service opened this pandora's box and they're the only ones who can close it.

What I truly hope for is that Aramark cleans up their act so that their current and future employees will be treated fairly, which in turn will allow them to provide a better experience for their guests. But I'm not niave enough to believe that will actually happen. So my more realistic hope is that the Park Service will tear up Aramark's contract and kick them out of Crater Lake.[1]

Please don't let this stop you from visiting this beautiful park, it really is worth seeing and experiencing. Just remember to pack a lunch.[2]

---

1 *Which they finally did!*
2 *I don't know what food supply company ExplorUS uses, but I did make a point to eat at the lodge before publishing this second edition, and I'm happy to report that my meal was delicious. I've also looked at the rest of their menu and it seems better than Aramark's, though still not up to the old standards that I mentioned at the end of Chapter 6.*

<u>BONUS CHAPTER</u>
THE END

As I mentioned near the beginning of this book, things only went from bad to worse after the 2019 season.

It even came to the attention of Oregon Senator Ron Wyden, who wrote this letter to the director of the National Park Service on December 8, 2023:

"I write to express my serious concerns about the unacceptable performance of Aramark, DBA Crater Lake Hospitality under its contract with the National Park Service to provide many of the services at Crater Lake National Park. I am alarmed by the serious failure of the concessionaire to fulfill its responsibility to provide

these services and the resulting harm to public safety, visitor experience and the irreplaceable resources in and around the park. Given the severity of these failings and the important role of the agency in holding concessionaires accountable, I ask that the National Park Service take immediate action to prevent concessionaire mismanagment from continuing to threaten Crater Lake National Park, its visitors, or the employees who live and work there.

As an Oregonian, I know you are well aware of the unique importance of Crater Lake. It is a crown jewel of Oregon – a volcanic caldera that holds the deepest lake in the United States. This natural wonder is one of the most pristine lakes on Earth and attracts visitors from across the world. As a national treasure, it was the fifth National Park in the country to be established and entrusted to the National Park Service for preservation. You have consistently demonstrated an awareness of this importance as Director of the National Park Service, and under your leadership significant investments have been made at Crater Lake

National Park, including safety and quality improvements to the iconic East Rim Drive. I seek to prevent failures under the service contract by Aramark from jeopardizing the important progress you have made on deferred maintenance using historic funds recently provided by Congress.

The annual concessionaire assessments paint a troubling picture of the concessionaire's fulfillment of its important responsibilities at Crater Lake National Park over several years. The National Park Service records make it clear that the concessionaire has continually failed to fulfill the requirements of the contract. Despite repeated and documented attempts by the National Park Service to secure performance, it is clear that little progress has been achieved to meaningfully resolve most of these serious issues.

After becoming aware of these issues, I directed my staff to conduct an in-person assessment of the conditions at facilities within Crater Lake National Park. The issues that staff observed during this visit have only served to solidify my understanding of the seriousness of the concessionaire's failure to plan for and perform important regular maintenance, adequately train staff and address issues that directly threaten safety.

It was apparent to my staff that the dedicated National Park Service staff were spending hours of their time trying to manage the situation, are deeply concerned with the safety issues for guests and employees, and share our values of protecting the park. I am grateful to the National Park Service staff for their dedication to our public lands. It is clear they have prevented the situation from becoming significantly worse through their efforts.

Under the management of Aramark, the condition of park facilities has significantly deteriorated due to a failure to perform contractually-required maintenance. During the in-person visit, my staff saw employee housing in a state of serious disrepair. The issues included staff rooms without working heaters, siding falling off the building, and a notable lack of security measures to protect employee safety. The latter of these is especially troubling given reports that serious assaults and other criminal activity has occurred in the dorms and no acceptable security measures have been implemented to increase security and privacy in dorms, bathrooms and showers. These substandard living conditions continue to threaten the safety of the workers and the repuation of the park, and must be addressed by the concessionaire immediately to ensure the health and wellbeing of the staff.

There have been at least three diesel spills in 2023 at contractor-managed facilities. The troubling response to these spills was a failure to follow proper spill procedures, lack of timely response, all highlighting the lack of staff training, which threaten park resources. For example, the diesel spill from tank failure at the Lodge was not handled in a timely manner. Additionally, the concessionaire's staff did not report the spill to the Oregon Department of Enviromental Quality, as was required. The failure to follow proper spill procedures made the size of the spill difficult to determine, requiring testing and soil sampling to prove no release. The Oregon Department of Enviromental Quality has also recommended sealing caps to keep water out and my staff verified that this had not been done yet at the time of their visit.

There are additional concerning examples of the concessionaire's lack of following proper procedures. For example, reports show ongoing safety issues with the concessionaire's staff failure to properly maintain fire alarm systems, including manually silencing fire alarms, without notifying the park fire department, which is a fire code violation and puts guests at risk by rendering the alarms not fully functional. Guests have their health and safety threatened by the Crater Lake Lodge Restaurant's disturbing record of repeated unsatisfactory public health inspections. This has included failure to store food at the proper temperatures, failing to meet basic standards of cleanliness, and the presence of flies in the kitchen from staff opening windows without screens.

THE END

Further, I am told the concessionaire has failed to provide documentation to the National Park Service that the kitchen staff have recieved the required food safety certifications.

Finally, the lack of investment and deferred maintenance by the concessionaire is concerning and has prevented progress on a number of maintenance and improvement projects that the National Park Service has approved. The 2022 annual report states that none of the Personal Property Improvement Program (PPIP) or Concession Facility Improvement Program (CFIP) projects have been fully executed, as is required by contract.

As a result of this lack of investment and a continued failure to protect their workers and act as proper stewards of our public lands, I strongly urge the National Park Service to take immediate action to make sure the contract is upheld or consider if a new contract might be more appropriate. I know you understand firsthand the severity of these issues and I am committed to working with you to resolve them as swiftly as possible."¹

I may not normally agree with Senator Wyden – in other areas – but I applaud him for writing this letter and making it public.

The Deputy Superintendent of Crater Lake National Park responded to the letter by saying that, *"The National Park Service is committed to providing high-quality visitor services, including those provided by concessioners."²*

Well then maybe they should stop granting contracts to Aramark. Just saying.

Speaking of Aramark, this was their response: *"We take these concerns very seriously, and the examples provided are not reflective of Aramark's standards. Additional investments are planned to address other important aspects of our operations, and we will continue to work closely with the National Park Service to improve the staff and visitor experience."³*

Well fortunetly the park service realized that

the best way to 'improve the staff and visitor experience' was to give Aramark the boot.

FIRST EDITION ACKNOWLEDGEMENTS

I want to thank my editor, Rhea, for helping my sentances run more smoothly, for prompting me to explain things better, and for pointing out that there is in fact no 'd' in refrigerator.

And I also want to thank my only patron for being willing to put money towards the publishing of this book.

SECOND EDITION ACKNOWLEDGEMENTS

This time around I want to thank my husband and fellow author, J.P. Biddlecome, for redesigning the cover, suggesting edits and additions, and rewriting the summary.

Be sure to check out his website:
jpbiddlecome.com

PLEASE LEAVE A REVIEW

I'm a relatively unknown author, and need all the support I can get to continue my writing journey. Please consider leaving a review for this book on Amazon, Barnes & Noble, or whatever retailer you bought it from. Or you can even leave one on Goodreads. It will help me out a lot! Thank you if you've already left a review, I really appreciate it!

ABOUT THE AUTHOR

Rebecca J. Bastian grew up in the woods of Southern Oregon where she now lives with her husband and a small menagerie of pets. She became a bookworm at a very young age and has dreamed of being an author for most of her life.

You can visit her website at:
rebecca-j-bastian.weebly.com

1. Ron Wyden, *crater_lake_letter.pdf*, Ron Wyden United States Senator for Oregon, December 8, 2023 (at: https://wyden.senate.gov/news/press-releases/us-senator-ron-wyden-addresses-national-park-services-intent-to terminate-crater-lake-concessionaire-contract) (downloaded July 7, 2024)
2. Jamie Hale, *Sen. Wyden blasts Crater Lake concessionaire over 'serious concerns' in the national*, Travel & Outdoors, OregonLive.com, Published: December 12, 2023, Updated: February 22, 2024 (at: https://www.oregonlive.com/travel/2023/12/sen-wyden-blasts-crater-lake-concessionaire-over-serious-concerns-in-the-national-park.html) (accessed July 7, 2024)
3. Ibid.

www.ingramcontent.com/pod-product-compliance
Lightning Source LLC
Chambersburg PA
CBHW070433010526
44118CB00014B/2021